Dave Learns Spanish

by Evelyn Rothstein

Illustrated by Elizabeth Uhlig

Marble House Editions

Published by Marble House Editions
96-09 66th Avenue (Suite 1D)
Rego Park, NY 11374
elizabeth.uhlig@yahoo.com
www.marble-house-editions.com

Library of Congress Cataloguing-in-Publication Data
Rothstein, Evelyn
Dave Learns Spanish/ by Evelyn Rothstein

Summary: An ambitious young man in 1920's New York seeks to better his life by learning Spanish and getting a clerical job in a Cuban sugar mill.

ISBN 978-0-9815345-8-9
Library of Congress Catalog Card Number 2010929561

Production Date: 06/07/10

Plant & Location: Printed by Everbest Printing Co. Ltd., Nansha, CHINA

Job & Batch #: 93000

To my father, Dave, who loved learning Spanish
and twenty other languages,

and

to the many Spanish-speaking students I had
the pleasure of working with in schools around
the country.

Table of Contents

1. WHICH WAY TO GO?

Dave was already eighteen years old and still didn't know what kind of job he could do to make enough money. He had been working since he was seven years old, first delivering flowers, then picking up pins in a tailor shop, and later working as a helper on a coal wagon. He had finished high school by going at night and working during the day, but now he was hoping to find a job he liked that would pay him **good** money.

On weekends when he didn't work, Dave would hang around with his friends on the Lower East Side of New York City and all of them would talk about the jobs they might have one day.

Ned, one of Dave's best friends, was already set. "I have an uncle in the butter and egg business. He has a small farm in New Jersey with

Coca Cola
S. Goldberg
Luncheonette
Sandwiches
Newspapers

chickens and a few cows. He said I could work for him selling eggs and butter from a pushcart. Then if I make enough money, I could open a small store, and Dave, maybe you could work in there with me."

But Dave didn't want to sell butter and eggs.

Murray, another good friend, was very excited about some news he had just received. "Hey, guys, listen to this! My mother's cousin Sam just got a job in a factory sewing pants. He told my mother that the boss needs pants pressers and that I could have a job by next week. You know, Dave, maybe you could come with me and we could be pants pressers together."

Dave pictured himself with an iron in his hands, pressing pants all day. "No, Murray, I don't want to be a pants presser."

Dave's friend Jack was going to work in his family's fruit stand. Abe was going to rent a pushcart and sell stockings, scarves, and gloves, which his mother would make at home on her sewing machine. "You could help me sell, Dave," Jack said. "You have a nice way with people and they would buy from you."

Dave thanked Jack but said, "No, a pushcart is not for me. And I really don't think I'm good at selling."

What a problem! *What can I do that I would like to do and also make* ***good*** *money?* Dave wondered.

Then one summer morning as the guys were hanging around talking about baseball and the great "Home Run King" Babe Ruth, Dave noticed some men pasting a sign on a large billboard. He stopped talking to his friends as he read, Learn.....Spanish....Get....a....job.....working.... in.... the.... Panama Canal....Good pay. Jobs.... also.... in.... Cuba.

Dave stopped listening to the talk about Babe Ruth. *A job in the Panama Canal or Cuba! Imagine that! Just by learning Spanish. I could really go places, see the world -- Argentina, Colombia, maybe Spain! There are lots of places where people speak Spanish.*

UNEEDA
BISCUITS
LEARN SPANISH AND
GET A GOOD JO
WORKING
THE
PA
CANAL

The signmaker kept adding more information:

Classes in Spanish Starting Soon.

Register Now at the Educational Alliance.

First Three Sessions <u>Free</u>!

"Hey, Dave! What are you looking at? You haven't said anything in ten minutes." It was Ned reminding Dave that they were supposed to be talking about Babe Ruth.

Dave came back from his thoughts about the sign. "Look at that sign, guys. We can all learn Spanish, get good jobs in the Panama Canal or Cuba or who knows where else! No pushcarts, no pants pressing, no butter and eggs. All we have to do is learn Spanish. And the first three lessons are free!"

2. A NEW ADVENTURE

The following week Dave led his friends to the Educational Alliance to start their Spanish lessons. The teacher introduced himself.

Me llamo Señor Goldberg. Soy su maestro de español y ustedes son mis estudiantes. Vamos a hablar solamente español durante la clase.

For ten minutes Señor Goldberg spoke only in Spanish. Then he pointed to the words he had written on the blackboard and asked everyone in the class:

Repitan después de mí. He pronounced each word and used his pointer to signal to the class to repeat what he had said.

Hola. ¿Cómo estás?

Estoy bien. ¿Y tú?

Muy bien, gracias.

AaBbCcDdEeFfGgHhIiJjKl
¡Hóla! ¿Cómo
está Vd?
¿Cómo se llama
Vd.?

It didn't take long before Ned put his head on the desk. Murray started doodling on a piece of paper, and Jack fell asleep. But Dave kept going with the teacher.

¿Qué tiempo hace?

Hace calor. Hace frío. Hay sol. Hace viento.

Dave was enjoying the class, but he was thinking, *This is slow. At this rate I'll never know enough Spanish to work in Panama or Cuba or anywhere.*

Ned was poking the other guys, signaling them to walk out. *They'll come back for the two other free lessons*, thought Dave. *Maybe it will get better.*

Dave's friends were waiting for him on the street. "I'd rather work in the North Pole than sit through that," said Jack.

"Give me a pushcart any day," grumbled Abe.

"Better to press pants for the rest of my life," hissed Murray.

"Do what you want, Dave," added Ned, "but don't drag us into that boring class. We'll live with what we've got."

Dave walked away, pondering what was next. *I'll go back to the class, and if that doesn't work, maybe I can study Spanish by myself.*

3. DAVE'S METHOD

Dave kept thinking about Spanish. He went to the library and took out a book about the Panama Canal and one on the history of Cuba. He then went to the reference section and looked at maps of each of the continents to see the countries where people speak Spanish. Here is what he found:

North America, Central America, and the Caribbean:

1. Cuba
2. Dominican Republic
3. Puerto Rico
4. Guatemala
5. Honduras
6. El Salvador
7. Nicaragua
8. Costa Rica
9. Panama

NORTH AMERICA, CENTRAL AMERICA, AND THE CARIBBEAN
MEXICO
10
GULF OF MEXICO
ATLANTIC OCEAN
PACIFIC OCEAN
1
2
3
4
5
6
7
8
9
CARIBBEAN SEA
S. AMERICA

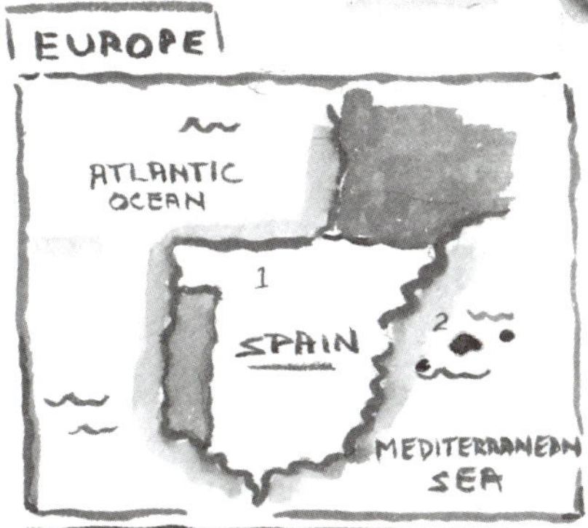
EUROPE
ATLANTIC OCEAN
1
SPAIN
2
MEDITERRANEAN SEA

S. AMERICA
1
2
3
4
5
6
7
8
9
SOUTH PACIFIC OCEAN
SOUTH ATLANTIC OCEAN

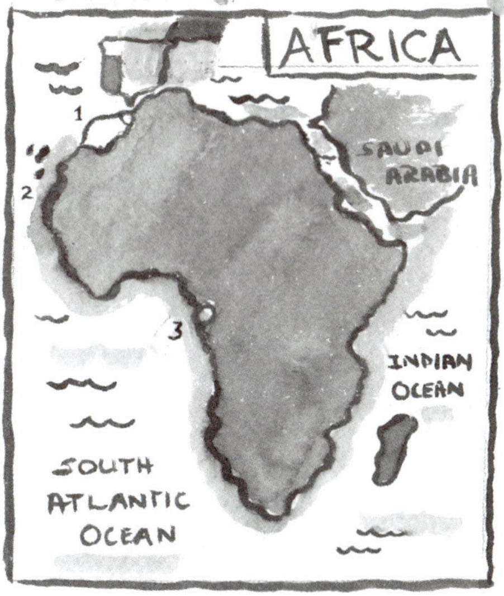
AFRICA
1
2
3
SAUDI ARABIA
INDIAN OCEAN
SOUTH ATLANTIC OCEAN

10. Mexico

South America:

1. Venezuela
2. Colombia
3. Ecuador
4. Peru
5. Bolivia
6. Chile
7. Paraguay
8. Argentina
9. Uruguay

Europe:

1. Spain
2. Balearic Islands: Mallorca, Minorca, Ibiza, Formentera, Cabrera

Africa:

1. Spanish Morocco

2. Canary Islands

3. Spanish Territories of the Gulf of Equatorial Guinea (today this is called *Equatorial Guinea*.)

I know I can get a good job if I learn this language, he thought.

A few days later, as he was browsing at a newsstand, Dave saw a newspaper written in Spanish called *La Prensa*. As he looked at the headline, Dave realized he could read many of the words because they were very similar to English words.

26 agosto 1920: **El senador Warren G. Harding de Ohio acepta la nominación para candidato republicano a la presidencia...**

I think one way I could start learning Spanish is by reading a Spanish newspaper, Dave thought. *Then I could look up the words I don't know in a Spanish-English dictionary.*

LA PRENSA
CIGARS
GUM
CANDY

So Dave bought *La Prensa* and walked to a secondhand bookstore a few blocks from his house. Just by chance, on one of the stands outside the store, he spotted a used Spanish-English, English-Spanish dictionary. It was only ten cents! *This is my lucky day,* he thought. *I've got to tell the guys! Maybe they'll change their minds and start learning Spanish with me.*

He walked back slowly to the candy store where he knew Ned and Jack and the others would be hanging out, probably still talking about Babe Ruth. As he walked, he kept reading *La Prensa,* finding lots of words he could recognize. He tried to pronounce them in his head so he would remember them.

La Oficina de Inmigración volvió a reducir el proceso de obtención de la ciudadanía este septiembre ...

He stopped reading and took a pencil out of his pocket. He then underlined *volvió* and *ciudadanía.*

When I get home I'll look up these words in my dictionary and then I'll be able to figure out the whole sentence, Dave said to himself.

Dave folded the newspaper, stuck it in his jacket pocket, and raced towards the candy store. *The guys will be really excited about this way to learn and, who knows, soon we'll all be hopping a boat to the Panama Canal or Cuba…or who knows where else?*

3. SPANISH OR BASEBALL?

Sure enough, there were Ned, Jack, Murray, Abe, and lots of other guys shouting and jumping and patting each other on the shoulder. The great Babe Ruth, the Sultan of Swat, had once again made history in Yankee Stadium. "Can you believe it?" cheered Ned. "He'll soon have fifty homers, maybe more!"

"I'll bet on sixty by the time the World Series is finished," added Abe.

"A million fans at Yankee Stadium. Who would'a thought?" came from Jack, who was poking everyone in the crowd.

Even Dave stopped thinking about Spanish right now because today, August 29, 1920, and into October, Babe Ruth would be the only thing to think about and talk about.

New York World-Telegram
7TH SPORTS
LATEST RACING
PRICE THREE CENTS
Babe Ruth Traded by Red Sox to Yankees for $125,000

* * *

That night Dave continued reading *La Prensa*, underlining the words he didn't understand and checking their meanings in the dictionary. He wrote all the new words in the small notepad he always carried with him. Then Dave had a thought: *I ought to buy a typewriter. If I can learn to type, I could copy the sentences from the newspaper, and then I can make up my own sentences*. He remembered seeing a sign the other day in a pawn shop for an Underwood typewriter that was only five dollars. *If I practice really hard, I might even become a high-speed typist. I definitely will make* ***good*** *money with Spanish and typing.*

Dave couldn't just hang out with the guys. He would soon have to find a job, any job, until he knew enough Spanish to go to the Panama Canal or Cuba. Reading *La Prensa* was a good idea, but Dave needed to hear people speaking Spanish so he could learn how to speak back to them. He didn't know anyone on the Lower East Side who spoke Spanish. His mother spoke Yiddish. Lots of the florists

PAWNBROKER
BEST PRICES+OFFERS!
FANCY GOODS · GOLD
WATCHES · CLOCKS
HABERDASHERY
WATCHES
$5

and construction workers spoke Italian. Many people were speaking German or Czech. But not Spanish. *There must be some neighborhood in New York City where people speak Spanish,* he thought.

Then one day Dave turned to the back of *La Prensa* and saw a section that said: *Noticias.*

Dave thought the word meant *notices,* but with the help of his dictionary he learned it meant *news*. He began to browse the news hoping to get some ideas about hearing Spanish and learning to speak it. Then the word *béisbol* popped out from the *noticias*. *"Béisbol, béisbol!"* he said aloud. "That's *baseball*. That's it. This is it! I can easily learn baseball words in Spanish." Dave tried to figure out the article with the help of his dictionary.

Béisbol - el domingo - en el parque ubicado en la Calle 110 con la Avenida Lexington. Una gran oportunidad para los aficionados que quieran mejorar su deporte. Todos son bienvenidos.

The next Sunday Dave took the elevated train to 110th Street and Lexington Avenue to watch a baseball game and hear the game played with Spanish words. *Maybe in a few weeks I can get invited to pitch a few balls,* he thought. *I'm a pretty good pitcher and if one of the teams likes me, I'll get to hear Spanish and even get to practice speaking.*

TO
DOWNTOWN
EXIT TO 111th ST
EXIT
EXIT

Dave took out his little notepad and wrote: *El Vocabulario del Béisbol,* and entered a few of the words he had found in his dictionary:

baseball player - *el pelotero*

pitcher - *el lanzador*

batter - *el bateador*

catcher - *el receptor*

to score - *anotar*

single - *el sencillo*

scoreboard - *la pizarra*

fielder - *el fílder*

bat – *el bate*

inning - *la entrada*

fly - *el flai*

ball - *la pelota*

Now I know some good ways to learn Spanish. I'm going to tell the guys about this system. Maybe they'll join me. But then, maybe they won't. In the meantime, I'm going to buy that typewriter and try to get a job as a typist.

5. THE MAGIC COMBINATION

Dave had been practicing typing and learning Spanish for three months. To make some money, he delivered groceries and flowers whenever he could, but he hardly made enough money for himself or to help his mother. Luckily, he was getting good at typing. He had memorized where the keys were and could type some practice sentences without looking at the keys or hitting the wrong ones. The book that came with typing instructions said to practice these two sentences to learn the keys:

The quick brown fox jumps over the lazy dog.

Now is the time for all good men to come to the aid of their party.

Dave knew that typing without mistakes was very important because there was no way to make any changes if you happened to hit

The quick brown fox jumps over the lazy dog.
Now is the time for all good men to come to
the aid of their party.
Underwood

the wrong keys. You would just have to type the whole page over again—and make NO mistakes.

Once Dave mastered typing in English, he began to type in Spanish.

```
Me llamo Dave.Soy americano.
Soy curioso y simpático.Estoy
aprendiendo español a mi manera,
y me gusta.
```

Then he would take the paper out of the typewriter and put in the accent marks with a pen because there were no accent marks on this typewriter.

I've got to show this to the guys, Dave said to himself. *They'll really be impressed and maybe now they'll want to learn Spanish.*

Dave read the baseball news in *La Prensa* every night, underlining the words he didn't know and looking up their meanings in the dictionary. News about Babe Ruth was always interesting, and one night Dave found this short article about him.

George Herman "Babe" Ruth es el mejor jugador a aparecer desde el estreno del béisbol. Ahora que es bateador para los Yankees, predecimos que se va a convertir en "El Rey del Jonrón." Está haciendo historia cada vez que batea la pelota y pronto será el jugador más estimado en la Liga Americana. ¡Gracias, Babe!

Dave understood most of the words. He was beginning to feel good about his Spanish and about his typing too. *I think that by next year I'll be ready to get a job in the Panama Canal or Cuba. I already saw in the "noticias" that there was a job in a sugar mill in Cuba for someone who can translate letters from Spanish into English. Imagine living in Cuba and being a translator. I'll be making good money and after two or three years in Cuba, maybe I'll be speaking Spanish like those men I saw playing baseball. I just wish some of the guys would learn Spanish so they could come with me. What's so good about selling butter and eggs or pressing pants?*

Every night Dave added more words and sentences to his notepad, then practiced his typing by translating English headlines into Spanish. Most of the headlines were about baseball, Dave's favorite sport.

Primera Emisión de la Serie Mundial,
13 octubre, 1921

Hoy, el estudio de emisión WJZ en Newark, New Jersey emitió por la primera vez la Serie Mundial de 1921. Tommy Cowan hizo la emisión de los juegos entre los Yankees de Nueva York y los Gigantes de Nueva York por medio de los relatos telefónicos que llegaron de los Polo Grounds en Manhattan.

First World Series Radio Broadcast,
October 13, 1921.

"Today radio station WJZ in Newark, New Jersey made the first broadcast of the 1921 World Series. Tommy Cowan broadcast the games between the New York Yankees and the New York Giants by getting reports by telephone from the Polo Grounds in Manhattan."

Sometimes Dave just translated articles that he thought were interesting.

¡Tome control de su dinero! Si usted sabe en qué gasta su dinero, le será más fácil pagar sus cuentas a tiempo, ahorrar dinero cada mes y lograr la independencia económica.

Take control of your money! If you know where your money is being spent, it will be much easier for you to pay your bills on time, save money every month, and achieve financial independence.

Para empezar, piense en la manera en que gasta su dinero. Debe destinar su dinero a la compra de cosas que necesita y cosas que desea, y a pagar sus deudas o a aumentar sus ahorros.

To start, think about how you are spending your money. You should direct your money toward things that you need and want, the payment of debts, or to increasing your savings.

Dave's plan to learn Spanish was working! Now all he needed was a job. He turned to the page with the *"noticias." Maybe there's still that job in the sugar mill in Cuba. I'm a pretty good typist and I think I'm ready to do some translations. Maybe, maybe...*

Right now, though, the 1921 World Series was on. The guys would all be hanging out at the candy store listening to the first baseball broadcasts between the New York Yankees and the New York Giants. And Babe Ruth would probably hit at least one home run. Dave put away his Spanish. Nothing right now was more important than the series.

6. A DOOR OPENS

By 1922, Dave knew a lot of Spanish. Once in a while he went up to 110th Street and got to play baseball. He was a good pitcher and the teams were glad to have him when one of their pitchers didn't show up.

¡Hola, Dave! ¿Puedes lanzar para nosotros hoy? Carlos tuvo que ir a Puerto Rico a visitar a su mamá, así que te necesitamos.

Muchas gracias. Sí, mi brazo se siente fuerte hoy y me gustaría ayudarles a que ustedes ganen.

But as good as it was to play baseball, Dave wanted a job. He searched *las noticias* every night, but nothing, *nada*. Then one day in October, on the *página de noticias,* Dave spotted the word **Cuba** among the words describing a job. In fact, there were two ads, one written in English and another one for the same job, written in Spanish.

HELP WANTED

Translator needed to work in the office of a sugar plantation and mill in the province of Ciego de Ávila, Cuba. Must be fluent in Spanish with good grammar skills in both Spanish and English. High-speed typing skills essential. Excellent pay and free room and board. Send letter of application in English and Spanish to:

Mr. Sanford Worthington, Central Dos Flores Sugar Mill, Tamarindo, Provincia de Ciego de Ávila, Cuba.

ANUNCIOS

Plantación e ingenio de azúcar en la provincia de Ciego de Ávila, Cuba, busca traductor para trabajar en nuestra oficina. Además de la fluencia en español e inglés, exigimos tanto un nivel alto de gramática como rapidez en dactilografía. Ofrecemos un buen salario y pensión completa. Responda por correo en español e inglés a:

Sr. Sanford Worthington, Central Dos Flores Sugar Mill Tamarindo, Provincia de Ciego de Ávila, Cuba.

Dave immediately wrote two letters to Mr. Worthington, one in Spanish and one in English, explaining how he had learned Spanish and typing. He promised to work hard and make sure his letters would be written in the finest Spanish and English with no grammatical, typing, or spelling mistakes. He then added that when he graduated from sixth grade he had won two awards, one for excellent grammar and a second for perfect spelling.

He put the letters in an envelope and addressed them in his neatest handwriting. Then he went to the post office to get the exact cost of postage, and sent the letters out.

Dave knew he would have to wait many weeks for an answer, but in the meantime he would buy a good Spanish grammar book and practice saying the verbs and then type them on his Underwood typewriter.

Dave ran to the candy store to tell the guys, but only Abe was there talking to someone Dave didn't know.

"Hey, Abe, where's everyone?"

"Where ya' been, Dave? Holding out on us?"

"I've been busy with Spanish and I just sent a letter to Cuba about a job. What's everyone doing?"

"I guess you haven't kept up with the news, Dave. Ned's moved to New Jersey to start selling butter and eggs. His brother told me

TELEPHONE
5¢
ICE CREAM
DRINK
Coca Co

he's doing great. And Murray's not pressing pants anymore."

"That's good," answered Dave.

"Yeah, he got promoted to a job working on a sewing machine. He told me there's still a job for pants pressing, Dave. How about going with me tomorrow? I think they want two guys."

"Thanks, Abe, but I think I'll wait till I get an answer from Cuba. Then I'll let you know."

Dave walked on. *I'll miss the guys,* he thought, *especially talking about baseball and Babe Ruth. But I'll just have to keep going with Spanish and maybe get that job in Cuba.*

7. TIME PASSES SLOWLY

Dave waited all through the winter of 1922 for an answer from the sugar mill. In the meantime, his Spanish was getting better. Every Sunday he went up to 110th Street where he had made two friends his age, Carlos and Miguel. They liked that Dave could speak some Spanish and were glad they could speak some English back to him. They usually spoke to Dave in *Spanglish,* a mixture of Spanish and English.

¡Hola, Dave! ¿Cómo está today?

Muy bien, Carlos, pero aún no me ha llegado la carta de Cuba.

Quizás mañana. Los cubanos están ocupados - too busy for *un americano,* Dave.

Es necessario que trabaje, Miguel. Tengo que ganar

OHNSON'S
QUID WAX
Drink Coca-Cola
CHLOROX
The Smooth Tooth Paste
ELGIN
5
PELHAM BAY LOCAL
TIMES
LA PRENSA
LADIES' HOME JOURNAL

dinero para ayudar a mi madre.

Then the conversation would turn to sports, always Dave's favorite subject.

If the day was cold or rainy, Miguel and Carlos would take out a deck of cards and invite Dave to join them for a game of penny poker in the hallway of their building. For two more hours, Dave could hear Spanish, learn words about poker, and have a good time with his new friends. His notepad soon had about a dozen poker words such as *los naipes, las barajas, los pares, el corazón, la pica, el diamante, el trébol, tres del mismo palo, el partido, una mano.*

Then before taking the elevated train back to the Lower East Side, Dave would stop at *una bodega* to buy some *fruta y legumbres*. By now, Señor Sanchez, *el propietario de la bodega*, knew Dave well and for a half an hour they would chat about *fruta, legumbres,* and also *béisbol*.

Hoy, Señor Dave, tengo los mangos más ricos y dulces. Y los plátanos están bien maduros y listos para freír y comer con picadillo. Tu mamá puede prepararlos para toda la familia. Muchas gracias.

Dave bought some mangos and bananas, hoping his mother would cook them. Then he and Señor Sanchez would talk about Babe Ruth and the New York Yankees.

Estoy seguro que éste será el mejor año para Babe. Aunque los Yankees no ganen el campeonato, Babe va a hacer más jonrones que ningún otro jugador.

Dave wanted the Yankees to win the Series, but Babe Ruth's homeruns were more important.

Each Sunday as he rode back on the elevated train, Dave would think, *If I ever get that job in Cuba, I'll really know Spanish.*

8. NEWS FROM CUBA

It was the first day of spring, 1922. Dave got home from delivering clothes for the tailor, opened the mailbox as he did every day, and.... yes, there was a letter with a Cuban postage stamp. It was addressed to Dave Bierman and had a return address from Mr. Sanford Worthington, Tamarindo, Provincia de Ciego de Ávila, Cuba.

Dave took a deep breath, afraid to open the letter in case it said, *Sorry, no job*. He walked up the five flights of stairs to his apartment and sat down on a chair in the kitchen, holding the unopened envelope and biting his lip. His mother walked in, kissed him on the head, and asked, "Why you so upset, Davy? You have got bad news?"

"Mama, speak good English! You've been in this country for over twenty years and you

speak like you just got off the boat!"

His mother moved away and came back with some milk and fresh-baked cookies.

"I'm sorry, Mama," Dave said. "I didn't mean to talk to you that way. I'm just nervous about opening this letter."

"So open it. If you got good news, I cook a good pot roast for you. And if you got bad news, I also cook a good pot roast." Dave smiled. He knew this was his mother's way of showing she loved him no matter what.

Then he opened the letter. His mother put her hand on his shoulder. She couldn't read the English, but she would know whether it was good or not good. Two minutes later, Dave was jumping up and down and hugging his mother. Then he made her sit down at the table so he could read her the letter.

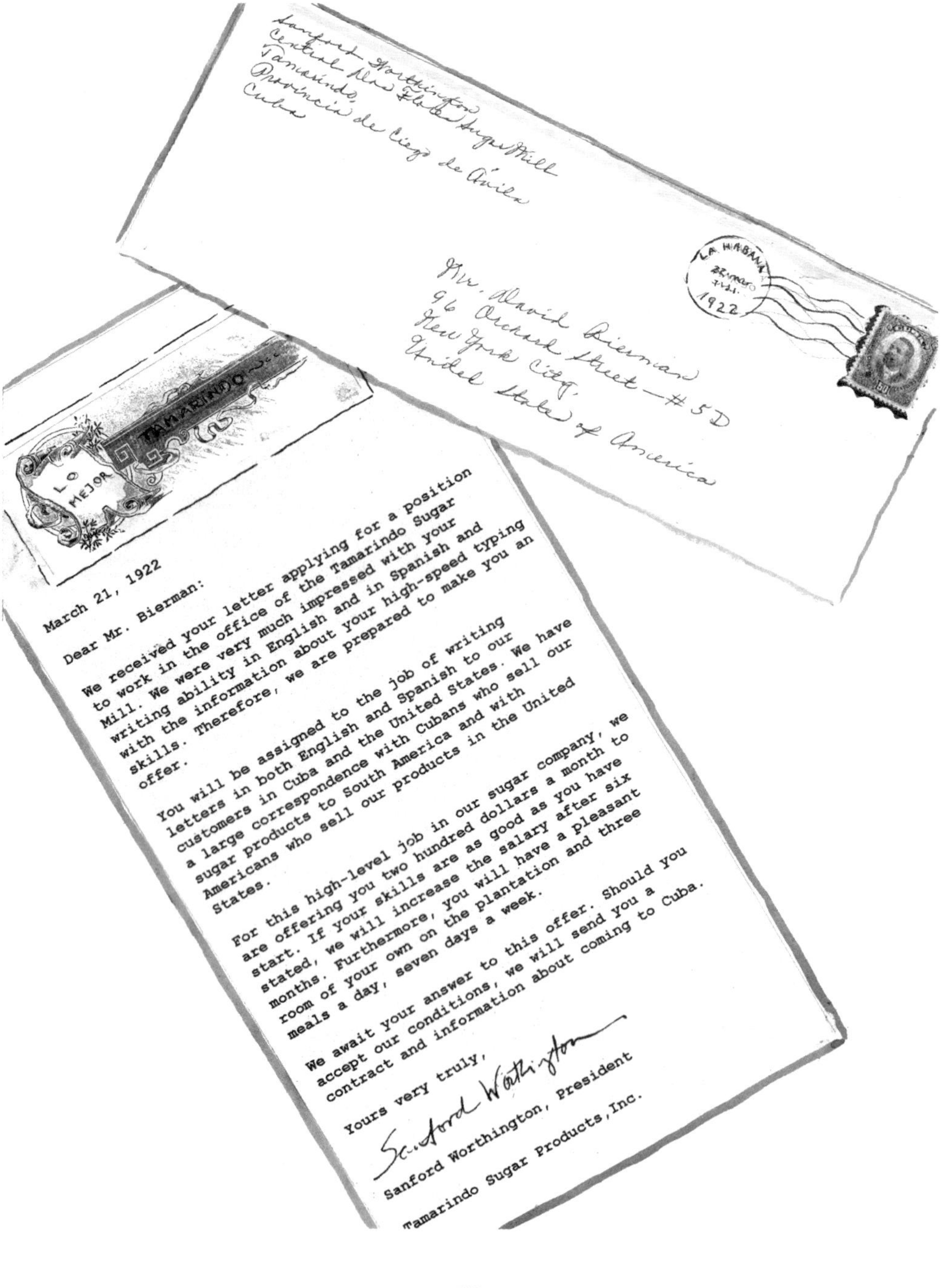

March 21, 1922

Dear Mr. Bierman:

We received your letter applying for a position to work in the office of the Tamarindo Sugar Mill. We were very much impressed with your writing ability in English and in Spanish and with the information about your high-speed typing skills. Therefore, we are prepared to make you an offer.

You will be assigned to the job of writing letters in both English and Spanish to our customers in Cuba and the United States. We have a large correspondence with Cubans who sell our sugar products to South America and with Americans who sell our products in the United States.

For this high-level job in our sugar company, we are offering you two hundred dollars a month to start. If your skills are as good as you have stated, we will increase the salary after six months. Furthermore, you will have a pleasant room of your own on the plantation and three meals a day, seven days a week.

We await your answer to this offer. Should you accept our conditions, we will send you a contract and information about coming to Cuba.

Yours very truly,

Sanford Worthington, President

Tamarindo Sugar Products, Inc.

Dave's mother was happy for him, but she then took out a handkerchief and dabbed her eyes. The letter meant that her son would soon be leaving for some faraway place, and she might never see him again.

* * *

Dave knew he was on his way to the future he had been dreaming of ever since he saw that sign about learning Spanish. Holding the precious letter in his hand, he dashed out of the apartment, down the stairs and to the candy store. *The guys will all envy me! They'll really be sorry they didn't study Spanish.*

But only Jack was at the candy store. "Where's everyone?" asked Dave.

"Where ya' been, Dave?" snapped Jack. "Murray just got promoted to chief pants operator with a good raise. Ned just told me he's opening a butter and egg store on Avenue C. Everyone's doing good. Even me. I got a night job in that new diner down the block."

Dave showed Jack the letter, explaining the good news. But Jack just shook his head. "You're doing a crazy thing, Dave," he said, "just when everyone here is doing good, and you could too!" But Dave was sure he was making the right choice.

As Dave walked home, he thought how glad he was that all his friends were working. And he would really miss them when he was in Cuba. But then he thought, *Learning Spanish is still a good idea. Who knows where it will take me?*

9. PLANTATION LIFE

For the next three months Dave was very busy getting his passport, buying a steamship ticket to Cuba, and saying goodbye to his friends. He was a little bit nervous about leaving his neighborhood and family, but he knew that going to work at the sugar mill in Cuba was a smart move.

On a steamy morning in July, after traveling for a month on a freighter, Dave got off the boat in *La Habana,* the capital city of Cuba. Everyone was speaking Spanish, of course. *This won't be easy,* he thought, *but at least I know enough to find my way and I'll really get practice in hearing and speaking Spanish.*

Dave took a look around. *In fact, La Habana is almost like where I learned Spanish in New York,* he observed. There were boys playing *béisbol.* Men with pushcarts were roasting spicy meats

ROME

with *frijoles*. Music floated out of doorways. *I like this place already*, he thought.

Luckily, Mr. Worthington had sent Dave the directions on how to get from *La Habana* to Tamarindo in *Ciego de Ávila*, first by train, then by bus, and finally by a horse-drawn wagon for the last ten miles.

* * *

Being on a sugar plantation was a big change from living in a crowded part of New York City. Dave's neighborhood back home was full of pushcarts and vendors and people jostling each other for space. The plantation had wide open spaces with endless fields of tall stalks of sugarcane. Workers were scattered here and there, and there was plenty of bright sun and blue sky.

JULIO
6

Every morning Dave would go to the plantation office to write and translate letters. Then he would walk around the plantation and talk to the workers. He was now speaking Spanish easily with the Cuban office staff and with all the workers who planted and cut the sugarcane.

One of Dave's best buddies was Alberto, whose job was to cut down the stems of the sugarcane, making sure not to damage the roots so that the cane would grow back next season. By talking with Alberto, Dave learned a lot about growing sugarcane, which would be processed to make the white sugar that he loved for sweetening his coffee and grapefruit.

- *Alberto, explícame, por favor, ¿cómo se saca el azúcar de estas cañas tan altas?*

In his mind, Dave was thinking of the words in English.

"Alberto, please explain to me how you get the sugar out of these tall canes."

- *Bueno, después de cortar la caña hasta la raíz, la llevamos al ingenio. Por eso, usamos los bueyes que tiran de las carretas a fin de llevar la caña cortada hasta el vagón del ferrocarril.*

"Well, after we cut the cane down to the roots, we take it to the mill. For that we use the oxen and carts to get the cut canes to a railway car."

- *¿Y qué pasa en el ingenio?*

"And what happens at the mill?"

- Eso es un gran trabajo. Pasamos la caña por un trituradora que saca el guarapo, eso es, el jugo dulce de la caña. Este jugo se hierve en una paila hasta que nos queden solamente los cristales de azúcar.

"That's a lot of work. We run the cane through a crusher, which gets the sweet juice out. Then the juice is boiled in a large pan until all that's left are the sugar crystals."

- Y el azúcar ya está listo?

"And then is the sugar ready?"

- No todavía, Dave. En el ingenio los obreros añaden a la mistura un poco de azúcar listo para acelerar el proceso de cristalización. Y entonces, colocan este azúcar en un centrifugadora a fin de sacar cualquier residuo de tierra. Finalmente, los obreros ponen los cristales al sol para secarlos.

"Not yet, Dave. In the mill, the workers throw in some prepared sugar to help the crystals form. Then this raw sugar is put into a giant spinner that takes out any dirt that might be left. Finally, the crystals are dried in the sun."

-¿Ya estamos listos a poner este azúcar en el café?

"So now we're ready to put the sugar in the coffee?"

- No, Dave. Lo que tenemos ahora es un azúcar viscoso prieto. Tenemos que limpiarlo y blanquearlo. No es lo que pondrías en tu café.

"No, Dave. All we have now is brown sticky sugar that has to cleaned and bleached. This is not what you'd put in your coffee."

- *¿Entonces qué pasa?*

"All right. So what's next?"

- *Tenemos que seguir extrayendo el líquido del azúcar prieto. Este líquido se llama melcocha.*

"We have to keep squeezing all the liquid out of this brown sugar. This liquid is called molasses."

- *¡Así se produce la melcocha! Cuando yo era escolar, nos daban pan untado con melcocha para el almuerzo. Éso es lo que comían los estudiantes pobres.*

"So *that's* how we get molasses! When I was a schoolboy, I would get molasses on bread for lunch. That's what they gave to the students who were poor."

- En Cuba también. Cuando sacamos la melcocha, lo que queda es el azúcar refinado, o blanco. Ahora ya la puedes echar en el café o en una toronja.

"In Cuba too. But once the molasses is squeezed out, the sugar that's left is white or we say 'refined.' Now you can put it in your coffee or on your grapefruit."

- Gracias, Alberto. Fue una gran explicación. Ahora vamos a jugar béisbol, y mañana regresaré a las traducciones.

"Thanks, Alberto. That was a great explanation. Now let's go and play some baseball. Tomorrow I'll get back to my translations."

When Dave returned to the office, he typed in English what he had learned from Alberto about sugar refining.

* * *

This afternoon Alberto explained to me how we
get the sugar from the tall canes. First, the
canes are cut down to the roots. After being
cut down, they are taken to the factory, first
by donkeys and carts and then onto a rail
wagon.
At the factory, the canes are put into big crushers
so that the sweet juice comes gushing out. Then the
juice is placed into a very large pan for boiling.
It boils until only the sugar crystals are left.
In the factory the workers throw in some already-
made sugar to help the sugar juice form crystals.
Then this sugar juice is put into a giant spinner
that takes out any dirt that might be in the
crystals. Finally the crystals are dried in the
sun.
All we have now is a brown sticky substance that
has to be made white. The factory workers keep
squeezing all the liquid out of the brown sugar.
This liquid is called molasses. When I heard this
story from Alberto, I remembered that how when I
was a little boy in school, I would get molasses
and bread for lunch. That's what they gave to us,
the poor children.
Alberto told me that in Cuba too, poor people used
molasses. Once the molasses is squeezed out, the
sugar that's left is white or, as we say,
'refined.' Now we can put coffee or on grapefruit.
After that great explanation, Alberto and I went to
play *béisbol* with some of the sugar cane workers.

Dave worked for the Tamarindo Sugar Company for three years. During that time, he became a skilled typist and translator who was able to speak Spanish to everyone on the plantation.

Then one day Dave began to think about going home to New York. *I haven't seen my mother or my sisters and brothers in so long. I really miss them.*

He also missed the guys and wondered what they were doing. *I guess learning Spanish wasn't for them. Maybe they really like what they are doing. Learning another language is not easy.*

Dave walked around the plantation, thinking, *I'll miss my amigos in Cuba. But I have to go home and start to be a translator there. I can learn Portuguese just as I learned Spanish. That should be easy now. Then I'll go to Brazil to practice Portuguese! After Brazil, I'll go to Argentina so I don't forget my Spanish. By knowing Spanish and Portuguese, I'll certainly be able to make good money as a translator. And then who knows?*

10. FULL CIRCLE

Dave arrived in New York by steamship in the winter of 1925. He had made enough money in Cuba to feel he could afford to take a taxi home from the New York harbor to his apartment on the Lower East Side. He was going to give his mother more money than she had ever seen in her whole life. And he would even share some of his earnings with his two sisters and two brothers. And then he would look for the guys.

When he walked in the door, his family was happy to see him. *Buenos días, Mamá,* Dave said. *¿Cómo estás?* Of course, his mother couldn't understand him and neither could his sisters and brothers. But they were glad he was home and were proud of what he had done. His mother prepared a tasty pot roast for him that night, and baked his favorite cookies.

“So what you think to do now, Davy?” his mother asked.

“I’ll first get a job as a typist in an office. That should be easy.”

“You make enough money doing.....that?”

“A typist, Mama, no. But I’ll start to do translations like I did in Cuba.”

“I don’t think I understand, Davy. But you smart and you know what to do.”

Dave soaked up the gravy from the pot roast with the delicious bread his mother had baked. Then he put a few cookies in his pocket and went out.

I have to find some of the guys. I wonder who’s around after three years…

Dave walked around Avenues A and B and C, the neighborhood that people were calling Alphabet City. He looked for the old hangouts where he and his friends used to gather to talk about baseball. When he got to the candy store, he saw a new owner. Dave asked him about Ned and Abe and the others, but the owner just shook his head. "Don't know them. Never heard of them."

Dave headed up Second Avenue, a wide street with lots of stores. *I think this is where Ned has his butter and egg store. If I find Ned, he'll have news about the other guys.*

Sure enough, three blocks later, Dave saw the sign:

NED'S FRESH BUTTER,

CHEESE, MILK AND EGGS

Eager to see his friend and get the news, Dave walked quickly into the store. It was busy with customers who were being served by a young woman. Dave waited patiently, and when the woman was free, he introduced himself. "I'm Dave, a friend of Ned's. Is he in the store?"

SORRY, WE'RE CLOSED

She smiled and answered, "Oh, Dave, you're Ned's friend who learned Spanish! Well, I'm his wife, Martha. Ned is out opening a second butter and egg store uptown. I'll tell him you stopped by."

"Thanks, Martha. Tell Ned I'll come by again soon. Oh, yes, tell him to say hello for me to the other guys."

Dave walked back home. *Tomorrow I'll find a job as a typist. Then I'll start sending out letters to big companies telling them about my skills as a translator of Spanish and…even Portuguese. I'll start studying Italian. That's not too different from Spanish and Portuguese. With three languages, or maybe more, I'll make good money.*

And then who knows? Maybe, I'll get married, have a family. Who knows?